BIRMINGHAM RIVER

By the same author:

The Ship's Orchestra (Fulcrum Press), 1966
Collected Poems 1968 (Fulcrum), 1968
Matrix (Fulcrum), 1971
The Cut Pages (Fulcrum), 1971
The Thing About Joe Sullivan (Carcanet), 1978
Poems 1955–1980 (Oxford University Press), 1980
A Furnace (OUP), 1986
Poems 1955–1987 (Oxford Poets), 1988

ROY FISHER

BIRMINGHAM RIVER

Oxford New York
OXFORD UNIVERSITY PRESS
1994

Oxford University Press, Walton Street, Oxford OX2 6DP
Oxford New York Toronto
Delhi Bombay Calcutta Madras Karachi
Kuala Lumpur Singapore Hong Kong Tokyo
Nairobi Dar es Salaam Cape Town
Melbourne Auckland Madrid
and associated companies in
Berlin Ibadan

Oxford is a trade mark of Oxford University Press

First published in Oxford Poets
as an Oxford University Press paperback 1994

British Library Cataloguing in Publication Data
Data available

Library of Congress Cataloging-in-Publication Data
Fisher, Rcy, 1930–
Birmingham River/Roy Fisher.
p. cm.—(Oxford poets)
I. Title. II. Series.
PR6056.I8B57 1994 821'.914—dc20 93–37267
ISBN 0–19–282342–6

1 3 5 7 9 10 8 6 4 2

Typeset by J&L Composition Ltd, Filey, North Yorkshire
Printed in Hong Kong

for Joyce

Acknowledgements

Many of these poems were first published or broadcast, sometimes in earlier versions, in the following magazines, anthologies and radio series: *Atlantic Review, Bête Noire, Catgut and Blossom, Circle Press Pamphlet Series* 1989, *Felt-Tipped Hosannas, First and Always, High on the Walls, Joe Soap's Canoe, Lettera, New Writing 2, New American Writing 8–9, Numbers, PN Review, Poetry Book Society Anthologies* 1989, 1990, 1991, 1992, *Poetry Now, Oasis, The Rialto, Shearsman, Stand.*

The *Six Texts for a Film* were commissioned for the documentary film *Birmingham's What I Think With*, made in 1991 for the Arts Council of Great Britain by Pallion Productions, producer and director Tom Pickard. *Anansi Company*, an artist's book by Ronald King with texts by Roy Fisher, was published in 1992 by Circle Press.

Contents

The Collection of Things

I encountered Sikelianos
unexpectedly, in the early evening.

It was in the bare, ungardened patch
around what must have been
his house, or summer place,
or his museum: shuttered,
builders' gear all about; a chained goat;
a telegraph post with a streetlamp slung from it;
Sikelianos
on his plinth in that scruffy, peaceful spot,
surveying the Gulf of Corinth
in the haze below, marble
head and shoulders a little grander
than human, flushed
by the sunset's glance across
Delphi's red-tiled roofs. He was
one more fact. Not a provocation
to any fervour, to any damage.

On a side track along the hill
there was damage: two bullet-holes,
small calibre,
crazing the glass front of a shrine,
erect kiosk of rusted
grey sheet iron, a worn offertory slot
under the locked, tended
display-case. Which contained,
undamaged, a green glass lamp,
oil for it in a pop-bottle,
a torn-out magazine page with a stained ikon.

And another place, below and behind
the poet's head, had a cracked gold
high-heeled slipper. It was an almost empty
grave under the cypresses, cut
shallow and dry in the churchyard rock,
most recently used, for a short spell,
by a woman of the generation

of Sikelianos. Nothing left in it
but the marker recording her death
at ninety, two or three years back,
and a plastic posy, some small bones, the shoe.

Sikelianos is gathered in,
called down from every corner of the air to condense
into that shape of marble, rendered to
a decent, conceivable size
and emitting among the hills a clear quiet
sunset tone that owes
no further obligation at all
to detail, description, the collection of things.

The Sidings at Drebkau

(September 1989)

By the road at Drebkau
the line copies itself sideways.

Parallel silent freight trains
stack themselves there
under a rolling low sky
that gleams on to the massed iron
and slides on over the plain
into Poland, levelling across
German villages with Polish names,
a forty-year-old border, a Poland
shakily written on a map of Germany.

Branch-lines that curve away
to the gas and coal combines of the hacked
forest and the flayed plain, haul out
brown coal to put a foundry-stink
into country towns, age them
brownish-grey, deaden their eyes
behind the scatter of cyclists, the school bus,
the row of flagpoles that hoist the community
a modest official height from the floor.

A land with the lights turned down,
hugging its powerless good sense to itself,
what governs it long since flaked away
into fantasy; this decency
won't leave an image bold enough
to be remembered by people who need it.

Even such image as there is
equivocates: simultaneity,
dilated out of nature by a monstrous
pair of hinged wars, seems to be dragging
some of us back through time to our lost, dirty cities;
yellow haze, poisonous rivers; home.

The House on the Border

Late on a summer evening the news comes blue,
blurred, brown, a transient green,
emitted more than received, the channel
left open for what could happen.

And the sun burns from the horizon
along the faraway carpark of, and into
the windows of a single-deck outlet for plastic
floor-covering, where all, for a few hours,
have left the chill cylinders deserted.

As the news wobbles, its mouths
sprawl and jig. The rooms hang
straight and dinner has turned out
to be restrained moist white
bread with firm cheese chunks
that carry a whiff and a kick. Nothing
to do but get it down, finish the day.

Far from their centres
two edges fuse, and backfill
the meadows that were between, levelling
dips, culverting streams, the streets
facing only inwards, walls closed on
bony bodies with soft skin, short
hasty bodies signed with unique hair.

Our Own

Bonaparte menaced our shores,
intent on poisoning the water;
the English, alone among nations,
climbed their cocklofts and slung
cisterns: 'Stop off the mains!'

And still today we keep our sovereign
tanks above us as we sleep,
trusting the bathwater
not, for a while, to blister us blue. But
Boney, thou shouldst, et cetera: our own
proprietors have had the waters
poisoned for profit, and have fought
Frenchmen for the right to keep them
foul enough to find buyers; with sovereignty
sold off already, they've nowhere
to fight from, and they're cracking.

So save us from our own
when the game's up and the profit gone

and the business all falls in
and back, and down, and bankrupt; when,

using contractual common sense
to correct the offence,

the Swede, the German and the Dane
make us buy back our acid rain.

A Sign Illuminated

In honour of something or other—poor
King Bertie's crowning; the Charter Centenary;
1938 as a whole—the city

decreed that on several occasions there should emerge
from the Depot on Kyotts Lake Road an Illuminated
Bus. On a published route

it would slowly glide through every
suburb and slum in turn. Crowds
might turn out. So it came

cruising on summer evenings, before
the little boys went to their beds, its lights
plain in the sun from as much as a mile off;

those lights were its headlamps and certain thin
patterns of domestic bulbs
all over the coachwork. What the city had picked

was one of its own
retired double-deckers. They'd sliced off the top,
blacked the windows, painted out the livery;

it was a vehicle so old
that the shadowy driver sat exposed above the engine
in an open cab. Among the little boys

were many who knew the design and the period
registration plates. In the sunset light
they could take it all in: this emblem

that trundled past all the stops; possessed no
route number, passengers or conductor; was less
than a bus, let alone less than lit up.

Promenade On Down

Against the crowds that push up from below,
their mouths the chief things about them,
teeth revealed, teeth covered, breath
taken and surrendered without advantage,
young men, young women, well-to-do. Downward

against the updraught and the bodies, one
civilised man with all his
appetites on him. On such a paper as this
there can be only one. More would turn
to a chorus, a clique, a college. Elated

all across his body, appetite
the seeds of coriander freed from their soapy
coating and the drooped foliage hung
dry above soil, appetite the varnish that tautens
wood lifted to the light. Passing then

by a god working out a term
as Exarch of the Steps, a blue stain all
about him. Air-blue above, deep
earth-blue under him. Most happy god!
He can take it. Propped on a lower level,

beached figure, aghast,
hollow with longing and old adventure.
Full heads float by, glance
at the live and the dying equitably. Padlocked
doorways, facades for rubble. Going on

down. Bearing up. Death's a shallow
box with a sound bottom, life's
the lid. Good to be riding its patterns,
incised, painted. Enlaced animals, shining
women, stuffed warriors. Twining plants

with flat leaves, printed
to give a harmless bitter taste. Or
breaking alive from knuckles in a wall
close by a pavement where many
poor popes go briskly about their business.

Photographers' Flowers

When old men get well-known again
and interviews come to the cottages,
the *dachas*, the garden corners,

there are pictures taken away:
well-known old men. Daylight
from the side and the hard old head
thinking about daylight. Silver
stubble, hands let still.

There's a secret that keeps them going.
Each has beside him at all
times, in a wineglass
or a scrubbed-out fishpaste jar,
his flower. That's how they stay alive,
quietly seated, each with his dried
seed head or spirited weed.

—So the photographers say;
searching the dresser for a glass,
the yard for a flower.

The Host

This memory, never mind what it is,
breaks in from nowhere with senses charged

and orders me to move over. Over
me it takes precedence. It's in flood.

Nobody but me has this memory. This
memory has nobody but me.

And for thirty-eight years eight months,
not subject, as I've been, to ageing,

it has lodged in me without ever
communicating with me in any way

I've recognized. There's nobody else
it can have been in touch with in all that while

except through me; and I know it's never tried.
Vampire memory, quietly feeding off me.

Going

When the dead in your generation are still few,
as they go, they reach back; for a while
they fill the whole place with themselves,
rummaging about, inquisitive,
turning everybody on; bringing
their eyes behind yours to make you see things for them.

Now there are more, more every year,
sometimes a month packed full with them
passing through, first dulled, preoccupied, and then
taken quickly to silence. And they're gone, that's all.

SIX TEXTS FOR A FILM

1 *Talking to Cameras*

Birmingham's what I think with.

It's not made for that sort of job,
but it's what they gave me.

As a means of thinking, it's a Brummagem
screwdriver. What that is,
is a medium-weight claw hammer
or something of the sort, employed
to drive a tapered woodscrew home
as if it were a nail.
                                        It's done
for lack of a nail, a screwdriver, a drill,
a bradawl, or the will to go looking.

The results come out mixed. It blunts
the screw-point, strains the shank,
bashes the head-slot flat. But
forced straight into the splitting wood,
it won't wind loose, and it can't
be twisted back out, even
if there's enough slot left for the bit.

It's instant, and it's obstinate,
and it's nobody else's future.
The screw dies in the attempt.
But you can be sure, if it's Birmingham,
that everything'll be altered
by the time you'd have wanted it again.
This isn't Yorkshire, or Paris.

—Eyes down, always down,
looking for the truth of it

fallen out of the air, out of
the vents of animals,

flaked from the skin of us all,
our pockets, the underparts of cars;

landlocked creeks
of dead ground, waste oil
with no dead river to float on.

Eyes down
for our own tracks, pressures of feet
that pack the soil down and mummify it:

lifeless trail, confirmed in
tarmac, concrete, crumbled and patched
causeways; innocence and habit

perpetually breaking the ways
across the earth, breaking the earth.

A zone of the air, ankle-high,
where dead stuff drops or hovers
in the taboo.

Dog zone,
shoe zone. Don't sit. Avoid
falling. Don't eat what's been dropped.

Disinfect dirty money if you find it.
Eyes down. Watch your step.

If you get systematic,
and follow power around, you arrive
at a bedrock out of a book. Sandstone
by Keuper, soft, so friable
it rubs back into sand under your thumb.

Exposed when the slopes need carving, it looks
imported, some sterile by-product
stuffed into the hills to swell them up.

The bald cliff of it that props the Jewellery Quarter
over the grandees' tombs gets concrete sheeting
to save it from the rain. Some bedrock.

Believe the Book of Bedrocks,
as, in the end, you must,
and you evolve Book City, just
as it evolved itself: rock, water,
forest, settlers, trade. Then
property, sewage, architects, poets.

Interesting. But what is it
when you're first set loose in it, with only
your nostrils, fingertips, ears, eyes
to teach you appetite and danger?

Is it the primal ocean, condemned
and petrified? Is it a giant
lagoon in Tartarus, petrified,
redeemed, made habitable?

There's one thing certain: this is
the centre of the universe.

The universe, we define
as that which is capable of having
a place like this for its centre.

There's no shame
in letting the world pivot
on your own patch. That's all a centre's for.

Anything else is politics: how far
West Bromwich is from London,
Handsworth from Rome, Sun
from his galactic vortex; Earl
Sterndale from Oxford; how far Clare
needed to walk
from High Beech back to Helpston.

Close by Apollo's
abandoned incinerator-house at Delphi,
its columns giving the air of a ruined
ironworks in the mountains,
I've held my hands to the displaced
Omphalos-stone, the single centre,

not of the planet, but of the earth's shifting
surface, the live map. To touch
the centre keeps everything round it
fluid, just as it did
when I still lived at ground level
and centred the universe
just beyond the mid-point of the garden path
of Seventy-Four Kentish Road, Handsworth.

This pair of big split pebbles set in the path
governed. Two, to be on the safe side—
I've always been a two-moon man. Keeping
a check on each other, rounded, odd-sized,
needing the company,
maybe they were the world's
testicles, or its nipples, or
its mismatched eyes, like mine; maybe its little
buttocks, or big toes. Playing safe,
and liking to feel at home wherever I live,
I keep them with me.

Again. What can it be?
A mountain with the wind knocked out of it,
fallen flat into its spread, wrinkled
skin, a wreckage in Nature,
with all its creatures forever
struggling out from under.

It's an artefact. A sculpture
a dozen and more miles across. Everything
that stands in it now
the work of one protracted
moment, an impulse to make;
a long century, the sort of time
it took to envisage and carry out
an unsigned medieval cathedral.

If a certain mind
could conceive that, and get it done,
the same goes for this work of art. It houses
a spirit that talks in ribbons
of tarmac and brickwork, puzzle-spaces for the people
to clamber on and spill through.

Either you run, or you face it. Compress
a shallow history to an act. Enquire who's there,
not signing. Inspect the signs. Eyes
down, for any lost clue.

What hand, what eye. Indeed. To have made
a work of art that's at the same time
the by-product of a spastic purpose,
oozing as miraculous drops
from a sort of spirit into a sort of matter,
gathering in pools, trickling to fill
wrinkles, indentations, then congealing as
masonry: factories, floods of houses,
shallowing as they spread, converted
again to spirit in the understanding. Spirit
filtered through brickwork. Counter-Nature,
caught into the sculpture and leased out
like the Nature that drips all down
the front of La Sagrada Familia.

The artist of the place
left plenty to chance, and time
and again got well served out. Who plays
in and out the tunnels? Who hangs in?

Seven hundred years ago
an earlier model of the idea, set up
on land above the Bull Ring by the proprietors,
did business as an Enterprise Park
for freed serfs. Similar rules apply.

And it stays centred
on the same spot, ignoring superseded
layouts and the quick turnover of the people; it holds
the inertia of an authoritative will.

The artwork's the figure of authority. Swung
on a green rail somewhere, with a low brick wall
under your feet, you hear
a moment in your life tell you that.

Ignore it; or go looking for it
behind all its names. Never
in the centre. Not the old centre,
nor any of the new ones. Suspect
repeated shifts of centre. The pace gets quicker.

The Forum of Augustus, sitting firm and new,
drawing centrality to itself,
had to have its back to a massive
curtain wall, set there to mask
slum tenements behind. That sort of place.

2 *Birmingham River*

Where's Birmingham river? Sunk.
Which river was it? Two. More or less.

History: we're on our tribal ground. When they
moved in from the Trent, the first English

entered the holdings and the bodies of the people
who called the waters that kept them alive

Tame, *the Dark River*; these English spread their works
southward then westward, then all ways

for thirty-odd miles, up to the damp tips of the thirty-odd
weak headwaters of the Tame. By all of the Tame

they settled, and sat, named themselves after it:
Tomsaetan. And back down at Tamworth, where the river

almost began to amount to something,
the Mercian kings kept their state. Dark

because there's hardly a still expanse of it
wide enough to catch the sky, the Dark River

mothered the Black Country and all but
vanished underneath it, seeping out from the low hills

by Dudley, by Upper Gornal, by Sedgley, by
Wolverhampton, by Bloxwich, dropping morosely

without a shelf or a race or a dip,
no more than a few feet every mile, fattened

a little from mean streams that join at
Tipton, Bilston, Willenhall, Darlaston,

Oldbury, Wednesbury. From Bescot
she oozes a border round Handsworth

where I was born, snakes through the flat
meadows that turned into Perry Barr,

passes through Witton, heading for the city
but never getting there. A couple of miles out

she catches the timeless, suspended
scent of Nechells and Saltley—coal gas,

sewage, smoke—turns and makes off
for Tamworth, caught on the right shoulder

by the wash that's run under Birmingham,
a slow, petty river with no memory of an ancient

name; a river called *Rea*, meaning *river*,
and misspelt at that. Before they merge

they're both steered straight, in channels
that force them clear of the gasworks. And the Tame

gets marched out of town in the policed calm
that hangs under the long legs of the M6.

These living rivers
turgidly watered the fields, gave

drink; drove low-powered mills, shoved
the Soho Works into motion, collected waste

and foul waters. Gave way to steam,
collected sewage, factory poisons. Gave way

to clean Welsh water, kept on collecting
typhoid. Sank out of sight

under streets, highways, the back walls of workshops;
collected metals, chemicals, aquicides. Ceased

to draw lines that weren't cancelled or unwanted; became
drains, with no part in anybody's plan.

3 Town World

Buckled and tilted a few degrees
this way and that, a plane

that runs always
to a horizon of roofs;

tarmac tracks
stamped through roof-slates;

tree-heads, ornate school chimneys
pushed high enough up to imagine over

to the next hard skyline,
border to another brick dish

with another covered river;
then over again to almost the same valley,

and past that to places that might look
the same but where *you'd*

be different; places where rumours start up
then crawl here on names without images; alien

factory-odours drawn up by the sun
and slid our way. Districts

with ancient buses; black air;
roadways of girders; concrete

visions in sunset dust. You'd never get home.

4 In the Repair Shop

The piano's a machine
hidden in a heavy piece of furniture.

As a machine, it's devised
to spill out infinities of notions

as a piece of furniture
it's a wardrobe, a cupboard, a house,

an hotel big enough
to hide every possible music

among corridors of blond wood,
passageways, staircases, all

ordained from the beginning, the sounds
buried like the veins in rock.

To play is to go searching in the keyboard;
to make music's to recognize what's found.

5 First Terms

Low
over infinite city
one urban sky that all its horizons share.

They'll tell you the place developed
like a coral-reef,
by millions of little responses and a few
major ones, cleansing its errors by the day.
The idea of a city. The ethical body. But
the empirical body's a unity: brittle,
slaggy lacework of roads, bastions,
breeding-cubicles, draped
on a thin armature of sewers
threaded with cabling and gas-mains.

Under that frame, nothing
you can sense, not even empty space.
Earth plots variously cut
in the floor: pitches, dog-walks machined
in tough grass: social soil.

Country's nothing but a single island
lapped in City, a benign
fistula where it all pulls open
by a few miles in every direction.

There, under different laws, a local Nature
hangs on, not even old,
just separate; its crumbling
dark brick barns and pitbanks,
looked down on from the sides
by cooling towers, an orphanage,
a fringe of houses. Deep
in that separateness, a ploughed field
makes heavy going to be with; equates itself
with an asphalt playground.
Hard court,
grass court; same game.

6 Abstracted Water

Abstracted water, captive for a while,
becomes abstract, a proposition in hydraulics,

slops through lock-machines, goes level,
carries coal, parties, makes money,

slides back into Nature, used. If it hadn't come
leaking out of the hills to be cornered

you could synthesize it: a float-medium,
liquid vermiculite, a thin gel

flavoured with diesel,
rust, warm discharges.

The Cut's a notion, an idea cleaner than a river,
and closed at both ends. It's venture-water.

The design depth doesn't allow for motor-bikes, or
layers of sunken gondolas from supermarkets;

Garbage In, Garbage Out. The boat called 'Heritage'
comes dredging. Nothing much fronts

the canal. Where buildings on a street
stare you out, here it's you who do the looking,

left in your peace a little way
from the backside of it all, among

blank, patched-up walls with huge
secrets that stink and flare,

piss out coloured suds. Secrets
half-guarded, absorbed; secrets forgotten,

left to decay, bursting apart,
letting the dead stuff spill out. Sunlight

under bridges stays enclosed,
lattices to and fro. There's a law

dirt grows out of.

The Poetry of Place

A resident of Rutherford, New Jersey,
happens to have for sale, at collectors'
price, a wheelbarrow,
old, but not old enough, red,
but too red: painting it up,
he's obviously not seen the shade
quite right. His greed makes him
a hasty reader. Glazed
with varnish, it'll do. Whoever buys it
gets to see the room where the original
things with ideas in them are.

Just Where to Draw the Line

A comment on Saul Bellow: 'It's marvellous—
I mean, just the little incidental descriptions
are better than most poetry. And they
just keep coming.'

—those Quattrocento paintings
with a tiny peacable city
on every hilltop in the distance
bobbing on the skyline in a rich
luminous watery twilight. While
near at hand huge imaginary personages
slug out needless religious nastiness
and mess up the view.

Poem Beginning with a Line by Josephine Clare

'The sun falls in sharp wedges inside
the room.'
('Morning')

The sun falls in sharp wedges inside
the night. When knowledge of darkness
and knowledge of day start moving
undeniably on separate
axles and slowly shake themselves
to bits that tumble back together,
new companies.

Time
hauling the time away,
fingernails windows of the spirit.

Within this ragged memory
I'm running the truth.

Top Down, Bottom Up

The neighbours' pair of goats,
lodging with us for a while,
breaking bounds,
supported the big horse-chestnut
as high as heraldry

could take them, and higher still,
erect on stretched hindlegs, throats
vertical, mouths upthrust, the pious
and guilty eyes oblique in their heads
as they ate the tree,

baring the white wood
to the curve of a back
patterned with progressed teethmarks;
ducking their skulls to force the bark-line
down to within an inch of the grass,

then once more rising, ripping
into the thick bark,
nibbling a tidy edge to the wound
and quietly subsiding with straight stares
though distant eye-slots.

The old tree, dying already from the top,
dies faster, with bolder strokes
that take whole branches out
to hang hooked up and bare to the sky

when all the others tip their fresh
leaves down by handfuls and lift
blossom-cones through the shade.

What's living rises by sinuous
rivers of lichened bark, inaccessibly
turned in the complex trunk,
too deep to be devoured; what's dead
comes reaching down to touch

with naked wood, sculpted and
signed by active young
goats, one already long dead
the other long gone away.

There'll be
years more of this, the worked object
altering passively as it must; a black
bough at a time,
a few more claws
clear of the canopy each spring.

SEVEN FIGURES FROM *ANANSI COMPANY*

1 *Dry Skull*

Just to be with you, I've been
getting myself ready.
Shaved my cheeks and chin
closer than close.

No trouble.

Now, we can always
be closer than close.

Trouble. Trouble.

2 *Chicken-Hawk*

It's the length of the drop
and the weight
and build of the client. For pay,
chickens are ideal. Thank you.

Three-and-a-quarter
seconds of wing-shadow
is the absolute
maximum the client experiences—
unless there's an intermediate
transportation element involved.

Yes, I do private commissions. Yes.
Transport and Dump? Ah,
Terrify, Transport and Dump.
I should think so. Distance times weight
times fright. Let me quote you.

3 Rabbit

Sidekick.   Other side
kick.   Sit still.   What's up?
Ears.   Can't
sleep with ears up,
never could, never will, not
my way.   There's nothing
up.   Odd.   Don't like it.   If
selected I won't run, because I won't
still be there.   If I was, I
would, though.   Kick up, dig
down, get under, kick back and
up and out.   Sidekick and
off.

4 Snake

See my head?   It's packed with
electronics.
It's the Service Module.

It goes wherever the Body
steers it
dangles it
slides it
in.   The lenses
are always open when not
shuttered.   The whole
capsule cranks back
to monitor the sky while the Body
feeds.

I can bite head, and
head, and head.   But can't
nobody never kick ass on *me*.

5 Tiger

Amateur dramatics, amateur
sport—one day
you professionals are going to give us a run
for our money. Call me Tim. What's
my profession? Oh,
call me a farmer. Of sorts.
Live off the land. Bit of this,
bit of that. Livestock, forestry . . .
Everybody knows me. So—
anything you need, just
mention my name. Belch. Excuse me.
Why not call me Tiny.

6 Parrot

YAM PRANK RAPPED
MAD YAMS LASH TOP CAT
SNAKE'S HEAD-BITE DODGE GOES TO POT
IS PARROT PRETTY BOY? NEW PROBE
THUMBS DOWN FOR SPIDER'S CAT-FLING BID
NOISE ROW: RAT-BATS HIT BACK
CHIMP 'CHUMS' SLAM TREE-TOP SEX-ROMP SLUR

NEW SKULL THREAT LOOMS
TOP CAT'S LOST NUTS: HOPES FADE
NEWSBIRD SAVES ANT FROM CHAT-SHOW HOST
HAWK'S 'JUST DROPPED IN' CLAIM QUIZZED
TIGER-TALE TALKS: FRESH TERMS
COURT TOLD OF BEES' TIGHT SQUEEZE

HUNT IS ON FOR KILLER STOOL
PARROT IN RAT-BAG SMEAR DENIAL
HAWK'S PLUMMETING SKULL FEAT
OWL: NUDE GRAN IN MERCY DASH
'I WAS DUPED' CLAIMS BEDROOM RABBIT
PARROT: NEW BISCUIT PLEA

ANGER OF TOPLESS MUM-TO-BE
HELP NEWSBIRD FIGHT OFF NEWS-FUN CRACKDOWN
PLUMMETING SKULL: FRESH FACTS
MEDIA BIRD SIGNS TOP BOOK DEAL: SPIDER TELLS ALL
BOOK TO REVEAL WEB PAIR'S ROMP SECRETS
TIGER DENIES HORSE CHARGE
FUNBIRD TO GET OWN SHOW—OFFICIAL

7 Cat

I say	my poem
to myself:	it goes,
'When hunger gnaws	remember that
Hope springs eternal	in the human cat.'
I turn	over
and say it	again.
And then I say	this one:
'In my	end is my
beginning.	In my eye
is my	arsehole.'
That's a	*lovely* poem.

Every Man His Own Eyebright

for Tony Baker

two-lipped, open-mouthed/
in general/
small, erect, slender or
robust annual/

variable low/ short
often bronze-green semi-parasitic/
late twentieth-
century English poet/ often described
as belonging to an aggregate
species/ hairy
annual/ one good reason for not
describing the species individually/

common on heaths and
dry fields/ for roy
fisher/ the lower lip three-lobed/
in very specialized

habitats/ purple lines on the lower
lip/a generalized description
would suit most of them/ quite
definite distributions/ unstalked
with a two-lipped corolla

characteristically marked with
a yellow spot/ derelict
industrial areas/ very
complex group/ favourite words:
or, if/ under
the two-lobed upper lip/
flowers, white, often tinged

with purple veins on a
yellow spot/ little
discernible forward movement
in the axils of the upper leaves/ the upper
lip with two reflexed lobes

and the lower lip with three
lobes/ favourite colours:
silver, grey, whitish/often
no more than six inches
high/ with white hairs on the stem/
as often as not in prose/

split up into a large
number of species difficult
to distinguish/ often well-
branched/ more or less oval,

deeply toothed, the upper sometimes
alternate/ perceptual scepticism/
with broad toothed bracts/

many species described would be unlikely
to be the one found by any one
person/ blue, violet
or white, and two-lipped/ further
complicated by the fact
that they often hybridize freely/
rust/ all look much alike/ fruit hairy

The Ticket-of-Leave Man

for Jonathan Williams

Jonathan, I dreamed last night of Basil Bunting,
four years dead but seeming
no worse than a bit drunk. It was for a pub lunch
in somebody's house he'd come back for an hour,
and to tell us about the play he'd been writing,
based, so he said, on a 'fragment of Chaucer—a *terzel'*
he'd doubtless made up himself. At a guess,
they'd been keeping him very short of people
he could talk to. One of us, a big fellow,
put an arm round the old man's shoulder. 'Nobody
would ever have tried *that* on
while he was alive,' I thought.

Homage to Edwin Morgan

When Scotland shall secede, and lift itself
clear of the yelping South, let the boundary
be drawn again with tact. There must be room
for the lately abandoned counties of England
and the defectors drifting north.
So have the southernmost frontier post
set at the bridge by Derby
where the '45 petered out. My house sits
forty miles to the north, so I can show
ways through Derby by back roads in darkness. Pay me
with sure asylum and a strong border;
don't let me go to London any more.
I know of *real* Scots Fishers; my first name
comes from the Gaelic. I'll learn to spell it.

And I invoke your gods. First, in his knobbly bowler,
the Burry Man at South Queensferry, then,
at the South Queen Mary Ferry—Burns!
The Merry Queen; the Whittrick (where
in Hell did *that* come in from ?)—Hey! Suddenly
there's a man at the Queen's south fur . . .

O furry Queen of Scots! McGonagall
should bring anew your softness to the breasts of Englishmen,
and respectfully remind you how our Buxton waters, gently
  mineral,
used to help your arthritis considerably, now and again.

Freelance

As always, it's the dreams that make the best sense of it:
powerful blasts from the base of the brain
send mind-litter scurrying for oblivion,
some of its tangles, for a chance of survival,
fusing into desperate narratives, the nearer
the knuckle the better the chance.
                                                                  Crick,
I'm relieved to be told they're nothing but
phantasms of disappearing waste, guaranteed
not to be meaningful.
                                          So I'm glad I'm not really
hired to take a class in Creative Writing
at a bus-stop in Barcelona; glad
I've not started up a winter-long Tuesday
WEA class in some far-flung hole in the night,
then forgotten to turn out for the next ten weeks;

and especially glad that I haven't after all
entered myself for a school exam
where a section of the English paper commands:
'Write a short sequence of poems. *Either*
a sequence entitled "Clean" (six poems)
or a sequence entitled "Dirty" (two poems only).'

English '88

Strong juices, smokes inhaled,
forced hyperventilations, drum-noise
peel back the shaman's brain and leave
clear passage for the gods to speak,
rasping and limited and low,
with magic voices they make up
in the hollow of his fled
human voice.

For years, the two
elect rulers of the English West
have also been divine. They've both been
out to the market and bought
special strange voices for telling us
special strange things, which no normal person
could utter. It's
what the people expect.

In the Visitors' Book

'Fish and parsley sauce got cooked
behind a first-floor landing door, some
hours before each visit. An unseen
neighbour would lay out scent-
trails of unease across the stairs
to mark the climb to something I knew
to be strange, however orderly. Up there,
clear hospital-inmate views down into
miniaturized garden strips with pools
while giant aircraft lunged
grey-bellied from behind the roof,
sagging on out of sight
towards a runway. Views, and talk,
friendly, but less inquisitive
than the ghost of the unknown woman's cooking.'

A Song

A song wiser than its words
cuts a wall out of nothing
with a jagged blade. Cuts it
clean, the jagged wall
to sit against, head lifted,
the song a glossary away, the voice
a substitute for smoking.

Not many sing
so narrow,
so wavering,
to the tune of a saw-cut.

A Working Devil for the Birthday of Coleman Hawkins

Night cities
rotating slowly,
nothing under them,
or above, or between.

Pillars
of darkness erect
cities laced with lights.
Dark tongues push down.

Head for where lights grow
in strings, in thickets;
feel for a pavement.

Not
unnatural: territory animal
slopes through the stacked
pens it constructs;
feeds from a factory district, drinks
from the still. Goes to bed
on floors of silver-fish.

Music built like a street,
tunnel of town breath
shifting with traffic. Heaviest
sounds leach out, slip down,
swill on the car floor,
booting back up through the seats and
into what weights them.

Plaited
in the music, in the long
twist of its slippery inner fold,
the agitation of pleasure, hard-working
stairway devil. All
the split-skirt, white-gartered
clan regalia: satin,
spray-on skin-tangs, more

than enough perfume to sweat into;
trembling, charged,
helpless with self.

Never far off, black mood
at how things ought to be: rough
freedom-guesses, mind-scours,
bodily energy
knocking itself out for folks
to marvel at, take heart from
and duck. Pleasure
a brush fire, feeding
on who's around, crackle of
static in scented hair. Wonderful
dangerous glitter; heavy self
gets sacrificed for the show,
hacks on, an urgent phone; overpass,
underpass, ringroad.

Steady. A roadhouse bar's a town
so long as the staff have
a jacket between them and nobody
comes by tractor. Shut out
the empty world. Settle. The spirit's
urban, right to the toecaps.

Hulk city. Streetlamp giants
stare in through tall dull windows,
shadowing a floor mattress
on or near whose corner
the kittens learn how to piss. Tough
sleep. Anyone can do this much.

Morning an uncleared head and a runway
ninety miles long to the next place,
with wagons, a built-in gale, grit.

Liberal inclinations
plaited into the music's leather
that's strong enough
to protect sprawls,
lurches, scratches, all
knees and whisky. Not every self
can help itself. Once more, let fly.

Day In, Day Out

Escapist realism,
flight for a day
on a determinist train,
the wear on the track tuned
to one fugitive's weight.

Likelihood
of a certain emotion at the flight's extremity;
great unlikelihood of its failure
to be conjurable: the mark
being that which the one available shot
can't but hit.

Given that,
a brake that drags and catches
scrapes a thin colour on to the certain emotion;
dresses it.

The Mark

Yet with no peace of mind
with clouded eyes and haunted
when pastures tilt as sunlit
sheets. Wind hitting low

What it is, milk, not white
but lifted to a shine
under the metal cup that clasps
a lamp on straggled flex

Orchards going down,
dark end of October.
A limp on the path between
byres and barns

By seeking about, slow hunt
by scent, sun in a cloth;
peace on a different tongue.
By wearing down

Squatting in bright blacklead
in the hearth, named a man,
faces the room, sputters,
smokes, won't satisfy

Why not utter a strange
notion, just as its minute
threatens to pass? A thing
that smells no advantage

but has to be spoken out
from special clothing,
heavy, fresh from the cupboard.
The thought is nobody's

Wearing down, worn down, worn
away. Other forms
inhabit the whole skin, abandon it,
struggle against air and die

Worn down. Brushing against health
harms it, a shove, a flush,
dragging, a discomfiture. Bought
in advance, with small change,

with walking away small time
nearly to nothing. Less
than could serve. The lamp
drilling away what's too little

Fallen out of calculation,
visible when remembered
the hour lies in the ground,
white body, pointing the way.

Upright

Narrow free-standing spire
dropping the whole way
from lifted kangaroo-head, its own
apex of intent,

to squat lightly into the earth,
an air machine,
pale stone chambers smelling
softly of law, puckers

that carry vibrations,
vulcanite to polished bone.
It need not obey
darkness, depth. It seeps

only evaporations,
needs no drain. A dream of
splendour designed it against us
before our time. It is all

given. A woman with rows of teeth,
lanky, sick, lonelier than mothers,
would call the children, make them take
presents they had to hide.

The Mouth of Shade

The mask behind the face
can't see: slants of dark
barely dividing puckered
lids. Wolf cheeks
sunk, taut, mouth fallen,
empty pit,
straight to the base of the lungs
whose pumped-out air
lets the mouth say what it likes
without closing. Talkative,
sure of itself by the minute, but
lacking memory; whatever comes
through next, from wherever.

How stale it sounds; how sudden
with life a moment later,
kicking down deep
into the shoe, knowing
the total ropes. Metallic
flash in the eye-slits,
then emptiness. What's left
in there to make it work?

A form. And the insignia, worn
nobody knows how long; hung loose
and comfortable, always kept fresh
for whatever the show turns out to be.

Three Stone Lintels at Eleven Steps

Low down in the tall
chimney-breast, sandstone-faced
with flakes taken up from the field
and cemented into a spread of kitsch,
a single working stone,
bridging the fire-hole as if it held
the house up free of the flames;
by way of work it also
decorates the blaze with a law and looks
almost as old as fire, the spare smoke
buffeting across it with a sooty stain.

Sign of a passage
through the field-wall that keeps
the sheep out of the garden; a long
ponderous dressed stone set level
just high enough for a man or a sheep
to crawl under it and out
through the opening, if there were one.
There's none. Nor has there ever been. Just
solid courses, below as above. The lintel lies
supported and easy, doing little
beyond directing the mind
strongly towards what is not.

The patch marked off as garden, finally
running down into disorder and peat-bog,
ends with a dry-stone wall, then
the moor carries on. Midway
in the wall sits a focus of all
the downwardness, gathering
as seeped waters intimate
in a knot of nettle and dock
that filters a cracked flood-drain and the ceaseless
trickle of the household, odourless after its
slow passage down through the tanks.
The puddle fills and flows over
through a roofed slot in the bottom of the wall
then straight out into the moor.
With the sun striking the stone and the lapwings

everywhere in the air above, an acrid
whiff blows back off the marsh
and across the wall and the lintel
that sits in its nettles,
taking the morning light like the cover
of a pure spring, but facing uphill.

Hypnopaedia

As I expounded *The Man With the Blue Guitar*
my students outwitted me.

Eyes glazed, or averted, they declined
to pick up a single question,
forcing me to drone on alone. I was so boring
I fell asleep.

Then a little way off
through the opaque white screens in my head
I started to make out a voice.
It was expounding *The Man With the Blue Guitar*.

Startled, I awoke, talking. Seven stanzas it had taught
without any prompting from me. Though curious,
I still didn't have enough gall
to check its performance from anybody's notes.

They Come Home

To win back the parents
from the passage-laws;
bring them home together,
bury them under a tree;

spread their bone-dust,
that now stares back at the sun
for the first time and not for long,
two colours of dry limestone,
female and male,
met for the first time, your
fingers and mine mixing your dead
in a layer across the topsoil,
set with corms,
aconite and crocus,
directly under a double-winged
trapdoor of live turf;

by no means separate the dead
from anything.

To have them
won back, by awkward custom;
lifted free
of the crematorium counter
and out from the poor
vestige of common ceremony;

left to our own devices, holding them,
each in a stout paper bag that
covers a squarefaced container
of dull plastic, coloured like
milky cocoa, with a toning beige lid.

And the last journey of all, of necessity
by way of the car-exhaust workshop;

they travel, your foot steadying them upright,
together on the floor, concentrated,
come down to owl-size in their jars,

and they stay there for an hour without us,
lifted up high on the greased, shining
hydraulic pillars under the workshop roof-lights,
closed in my grey-green car
while its rusted and burnt-out piping gets
yanked off and replaced. They come home
over a new smell of hot metal.

By no means separate
from anything at all.

Jars and their paper bags,
name-labels,
go to the bin, with the clearings-out
from the discontinued kitchen;

each has still
a whisper of human dust that
clings to the plastic,
the boundary a mad
regress beyond the microscopic.

They're going again in a day or two:

to be in part twice-burned
in city flames; eight hundred
degrees of the lance-burner
under the oven's
brick arch, and then whatever
blast of the municipality
lifts the remainder haze clear of Sheffield
and over the North Sea.

Envoi

At nineteen, suspecting my living might depend on it,
I started pretending to be grown up.

On my sixtieth birthday, suspecting there might be
unhealthy truth in Vonnegut's admonition,
we become what we pretend to be,
I kissed the pretence goodbye.

Whereupon
people I loved found it easy to give me toys,
while others, pleading the nation's poverty,
found themselves suspiciously unable
to find me money any longer.

Madam or Sir,
I beg you, turn out your toys and convert them
to cash for the reasonable hire of your poet. (Unless
you prefer to provide your own, exposed rhymes carry
a small additional charge. Metres come free.)

OXFORD POETS

Fleur Adcock
Moniza Alvi
Kamau Brathwaite
Joseph Brodsky
Basil Bunting
Daniela Crăsnaru
W. H. Davies
Michael Donaghy
Keith Douglas
D. J. Enright
Roy Fisher
Ivor Gurney
David Harsent
Gwen Harwood
Anthony Hecht
Zbigniew Herbert
Thomas Kinsella
Brad Leithauser
Derek Mahon
Jamie McKendrick
Sean O'Brien
Peter Porter
Craig Raine
Zsuzsa Rakovszky
Henry Reed
Christopher Reid
Stephen Romer
Carole Satyamurti
Peter Scupham
Jo Shapcott
Penelope Shuttle
Anne Stevenson
George Szirtes
Grete Tartler
Edward Thomas
Charles Tomlinson
Marina Tsvetaeva
Chris Wallace-Crabbe
Hugo Williams